INDUSTRIAL RAILWAYS OF THE SOUTH-EAST

Compiled on behalf of the Amberley Chalk Pits Museum by Ian Dean, Andrew Neale and David Smith.

First published 1984.

ISBN 0 906520 09 6

Text © Chalk Pits Museum 1984

Phototypeset by   CitySet Ltd, Chichester.

Published by   Middleton Press
                Easebourne Lane
                Midhurst, West Sussex.
                GU29 9AZ

Printed & bound by   Biddles Ltd.,
                       Guildford and Kings Lynn.

Foreword by Hon. W. McAlpine

From The Hon. William McAlpine

40, Bernard Street, London, WC1N 1LG

Industrial railways have a long history lasting back many years before George Stephenson's Liverpool & Manchester Railway. However, interest in them has always taken a poor second place to main line railways and even country branch lines.

Most books on the subject concentrate on steam traction in the few years during which British Railways were running steam down, but when there was still plenty to be seen in industry.

It is therefore all the more pleasing to be asked by the Chalk Pits Museum to write this Foreward to a book which covers a much longer period and wide variety of traction.

Bill McAlpine

INDEX TO SECTIONS

INDEX OF PLACES

PREFACE

For the purposes of this book, the South East of England has been taken to mean south of the River Thames and east of the London to Southampton railway; this includes Kent, Surrey, East and West Sussex, eastern Hampshire, and South London.

The Narrow Gauge & Industrial Railway Collection of the Chalk Pits Museum aims to make a permanent record, for the benefit of the public, of the narrow gauge railways of the British Isles and the Industrial railways of the south east. This record takes the form of full size exhibits (operational where possible), relics, documents and books, and photo-graphs. We are always interested in obtaining more of this type of material; photographs and documents can easily be copied and returned. If possible, a second volume of "Industrial Railways of the South East" could be the result.

Amberley Chalk Pits Museum
Houghton Bridge
Amberley
Arundel
West Sussex
BN18 9LT
Tel: Bury (079 881) 370

ACKNOWLEDGEMENTS

The photographic prints used in this book have come from the Library of the Chalk Pits Museum (which so far as industrial railways are concerned, consists largely of the collection of the Brockham Museum, recently amalgamated with the Chalk Pits), and from the personal collections of the compilers. The work of numerous photog-raphers (many of them unknown) is represented, but one person, Frank Jones, must be singled out for thanks, because his extensive collection of photographs, many of his own taking, has provided the majority of the early views in this book. Other photo-graphers are acknowledged in the relevant caption.

INTRODUCTION

by Andrew Neale

This is an album of the "other railways" of South East England. Those lines of varying gauge and motive power that were not or still are not part of the national railway network as most people know it, but served factories and gravel pits, gas works and paper mills, moving raw materials or finished products to the nearest main line rail head, river wharf or processing plant, or simply from one part of a works to another. Industrial railways such as these have rarely carried passengers, and on the odd system which did, this has invariably been purely the concern's own employees and never a public service of any sort. Until relatively recent times, very few railway enthusiasts took any notice of these railways, but with the ending of steam haulage on BR, the realisation that steam locomotives could still be seen working on industrial railways brought a sudden flood of visitors that would have seemed inconceivable a few years earlier. With this increased interest has come a spate of articles and albums, but these have tended to concentrate on those steam worked systems that have survived until recently. It is hoped that this book, which gives a far wider coverage of a specific area, both in terms of the period dealt with, the range of motive power illustrated, and the inclusion of pictures of the systems themselves, will fulfil a real need.

The area's first industrial railway was, like its numerous counterparts further north, a tramroad carrying minerals to the nearest navigable waterway. Of 3ft 6in gauge, it was built about 1804 to link chalk quarries at Purfleet owned by Mr Whitbread of brewing fame, with a wharf on the River Thames. It was another sixty years before locomotive worked industrial railways as we know them began to develop. Again it was the carriage of chalk that provided the key, this time from quarries in the North Downs for the newly developing Portland Cement industry. Indeed as the South East almost entirely lacks any coal or steel industry, which are the traditional strongholds of industrial railways, it was the cement industry which came to dominate the scene.

In the early days of the cement industry, transport of the finished product was usually by water and not by rail, so the choice of gauge for the works railway was purely arbitrary, various gauges from 3ft 6in upwards, including 3ft 8½in, 3ft 9½in and 4ft 3in being used. Like the North Wales slate quarries with the DeWinton locomotive and the Lancashire glassworks with the Borrows well tank, the Kent cement works had their own peculiar design of locally produced steam locomotive associated with them. Thomas Aveling of Rochester had pioneered the development of the traction engine, and in 1865 commenced building a rail mounted version of this. The earliest examples were simply a traction engine on flanged wheels, at first chain driven onto the larger rear wheel and later geared. Later examples developed more on conventional railway practice with a proper underframe on four wheels of equal size with stabilizing rods (resembling normal coupling rods) between the wheel centres. The end result was a rugged, simple locomotive well able to cope with the poorly maintained track, heavy loads and steep gradients that characterised the chalk quarry lines, where speed was of little or no consequence. The tale is told of Aveling's sales representative who visited Lee's cement works at Halling to discuss their order for a new locomotive. Lee's manager was a notoriously short tempered individual who was blessed with a wooden leg. When asked what speed he wanted from his new locomotive he shouted "Make it no faster than I can d—— well walk!"

If the cement industry was the largest user of steam worked industrial railways, it was by no means the only one. Gasworks and power stations were once major industrial locomotive owners, particularly the latter where there was not only a flow of coal inwards but consignments of coke, tar and other by-products outwards as well. East Greenwich gasworks rail system was particularly big with around twenty locomotives, a large wagon fleet, a large and well-equipped running shed and signalling controlled by gantry-mounted signal boxes.

Other significant users of industrial railways included paper mills, engineering works and particularly the military. Within the area covered by this book were the Longmoor Military Railway, Chatham and Portsmouth Dockyards, the enormous system that once served Woolwich Arsenal, the short-lived Davington Light Railway near Faversham, and the rather better known Chattenden & Upnor line. The latter started life as a test bed for various military railway ideas. These included a side tank loco that could be unbolted into two halves for easy (?) transport, locomotives with various experimental fittings, and several early internal combustion locos, some of which were moderately successful and others that most certainly were not.

After the Navy took over in 1905, things quietened down a little, but right up to closure in 1961 it was a fascinating place. A diesel-hauled passenger service ran for the staff and the odd visiting enthusiast who could scrounge a ride, while shunting at the various depots was undertaken by a fleet of centre cab battery-electric locomotives.

So far, we have only mentioned the more conventional industrial railways but there were also the vast number of little narrow gauge lines usually, but not always, of two foot gauge which served the South East's innumerable brickworks, sand, gravel and clay pits, limeworks, sewage works and factories. Few of these ever owned steam locomotives, the earlier ones being hand or horse worked, while after World War I the advent of cheap, mass produced petrol and later diesel locomotives soon made steam uneconomic in most circumstances. The exact number of these railways is not, and probably never will be, known, but certain areas in the South East, notably along the Thames estuary from Rainham to Faversham, were once an absolute cat's cradle of such lines.

Apart from the permanent railways discussed above, temporary contractor's railways for the movement of spoil and building materials were formerly a commonplace sight. In these days when the use of dumper trucks and tipper lorries is almost universal, it is difficult to realise that not so long ago any construction job of any significance would have involved first building a temporary railway. The heyday of such lines was the period up to 1914, when most contractors of any size would own anything from one or two to over one hundred steam locomotives, usually saddletanks of standard or 3ft 0in gauge, which would be moved from site to site as work dictated.

Not that the use of these railways ceased with the 1914-18 war, but it had a most significant effect. During that conflict, both sides made extensive use of 2ft 0in (or 60cm) gauge light railways behind the trenches, and the mass production of small petrol locomotives, particularly by Motor Rail ("Simplex") of Bedford (originally of Lewes), began in earnest. Hostilities over, all this surplus material was released onto the market, and 2ft 0in soon replaced 3ft 0in as the primary gauge for industrial and contracting uses. Major works employing contractors lines during the inter-war period included the construction of the Southern Railway's Wimbledon to Sutton and Chessington South branches, the big LCC estates at St Helier and Becontree, and large road construction jobs such as the Kingston, Sutton, Guildford and Caterham by-passes.

Working on an industrial railway was never a sinecure. Long hours and low pay were universal, while with the exception of some large systems, operating facilities were simple if not downright primitive. Some lines never even possessed a proper locomotive shed, simply stabling locomotives in the open air, or under a convenient lean-to or overbridge. The concept of "one man one job" was unknown, the locomotive driver often being responsible for maintaining his own locomotive, or at least assisting the works fitter with major repairs. A compensating factor was the ready availability of spare parts from the locomotive's builder. Just how good this service was, and the ability of the main line railways to deliver can be judged by the fact that in 1912, the manager of a Kentish cement works should think it quite reasonable to complain bitterly to the Hunslet Engine Co in Leeds of poor service. Apparently, it had taken over 28 hours from the despatch of his telegram before some urgently needed parts arrived. Any readers involved with plant maintenance today might be forgiven for muttering something about progress when reading this!

It will be noticed that most of this introduction has had to be written in the past tense, and indeed the industrial railway, particularly the narrow gauge one, is a dwindling species. There are many reasons for this. Except for specialised jobs such as tunnelling, mining and transport over soft ground such as peat bogs, it is generally more economical to use conveyor belts or road vehicles than a narrow gauge line. Standard gauge systems have been affected both by the decline in rail transport generally, and by reasons specific to the industries the railways serve. The change in manufacturing town gas from coal carbonisation to "reforming" naptha, reduced gasworks rail traffic to the odd trainload of oil tankers, and the subsequent conversion to natural gas has left the UK with only two gasworks with very infrequent rail traffic, these being at Portsmouth, in our area, and at Avonmouth. In general the electricity and cement industries have remained faithful to rail, but the trend towards a few very large works and the handling of rail traffic in complete train loads, usually on the merry-go-round basis, have drastically reduced the need for industrial locomotives. There are now less than a dozen power stations and cement works locomotives in the area covered by this book, compared with the fifty odd in the cement, gas and electricity industries twenty years ago, which is in turn a fraction of the total existing fifty years ago. Major standard gauge industrial systems left include BP's Isle of Grain Oil Refinery, British Gypsum at Mountfield, and a number of locations handling steel, coal, scrap, cement, paper and military traffic of various kinds. Industrial narrow gauge held out for longer in the South East than elsewhere, but the last few years have seen a number of casualties, and the number of working lines left is well down into single figures.

Fortunately, this decline has been matched by a corresponding interest in preservation, and in recent years few interesting locomotives have not been saved from the scrapyard, although on the debit side, it is now worrying how sadly neglected are many "preserved" industrial steam locomotives, whilst historic diesel and petrol locomotives are regarded as mere workhorses to be modified or cut up as the needs or whims of their owners dictate.

A pioneer of a more constructive approach to industrial narrow gauge preservation was the Brockham Museum near Dorking, Surrey. Founded by a group of members of the Narrow Gauge Railway Society in 1962, it was situated in part of the former Brockham Limeworks. At that time few enthusiasts had the slightest interest in narrow gauge IC locomotives, and even steam locomotives changed hands for a small fraction of what they do now. Although finance and support has always been small, thanks to a great deal of effort by those few and the generosity of so many of the former industrial owners, an impressive collection of narrow gauge steam, battery electric, and early petrol and diesel locomotives has been built up, as well as numerous items of rolling stock, trackwork and smaller relics. Increasing problems with security of tenure and access to the site made the Brockham Museum Trustees decide in 1981 to merge the collection with the Chalk Pits Museum, situated on the site of the former Pepper's Limeworks at Amberley in Sussex. What might have been the sad end of a brave idea has in fact become the start of a new opportunity to demonstrate passenger and industrial narrow gauge railways in the context of the industries they served, and in the two years since the move was agreed, progress has been gratifyingly rapid.

All royalties from the sale of this book will be devoted to the building up of the Chalk Pits Museum "Narrow Gauge and Industrial Railway Collection". If reading this book has made you keen to support financially or physically the Chalk Pits Museum's aims, or simply visit us to find out more, then all the effort put into researching, writing and producing this book will have been well worth while.

BROCKHAM, SURREY,

With Siding to the S.E. & C. Railway.

Catalogue of the whole of the

BRICK-MAKING PLANT

INCLUDING

Brickmaking Machines by Whitaker & Co., Wire Cut Machines,
Grinding Mills with Elevators,

STEAM ENGINE AND MACHINERY,

20 H.P. ENGINE by Clayton & Shuttleworth,

WITH TRAVELLING WHEELS,

6 H.P. VERTICAL ENGINE by Garret & Son,

Shafting, Driving Wheels, &c., Pumps, 2 Brick Presses, Iron
Winding Gear,

LEATHER AND OTHER DRIVING BANDS,

Railway Track & Narrow Gauge Ditto & Waggons,

TRADE BUILDINGS

*13 Circular Kilns, Brick Shaft 100-ft. high, Machine and other
Sheds, Portable Offices, Barrows, Trucks, Implements, large
quantity Old Iron, and about*

350,000 BRICKS,

and numerous other items appertaining to the Business, which Messrs.

PEAT & HOLDSWORTH

are favoured with instructions from the Directors of the Brockham Brick
Company, Limited, to sell by Auction on the Premises, about 1½ miles from
Betchworth Station, in consequence of the lease of this yard having expired,

On MONDAY, 10th OCTOBER, 1910,

At 12 o'clock precisely.

May be Viewed during week prior to the Sale.

Catalogues may be obtained of the Secretary of the Brockham Brick
Company, Limited, Betchworth, and of

Messrs. PEAT & HOLDSWORTH,

Auctioneers, Reigate & Redhill, Surrey.

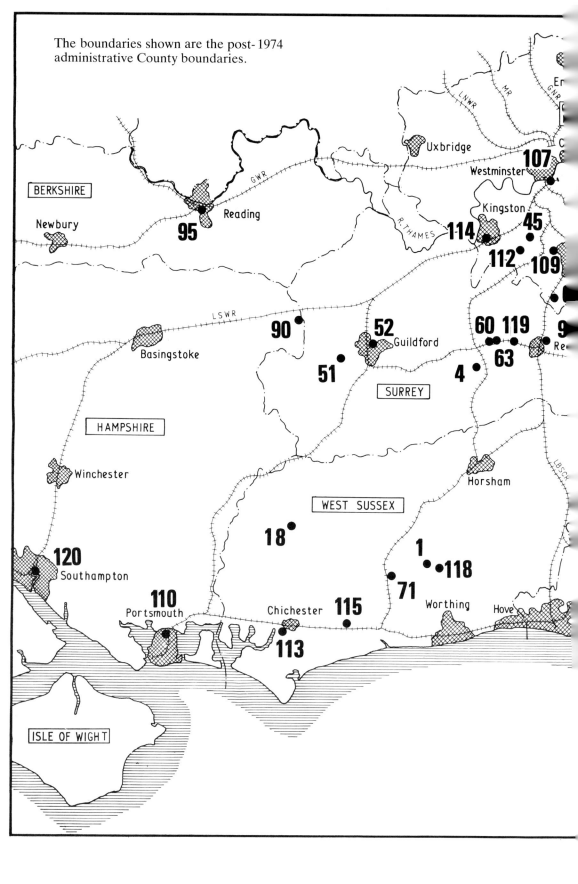

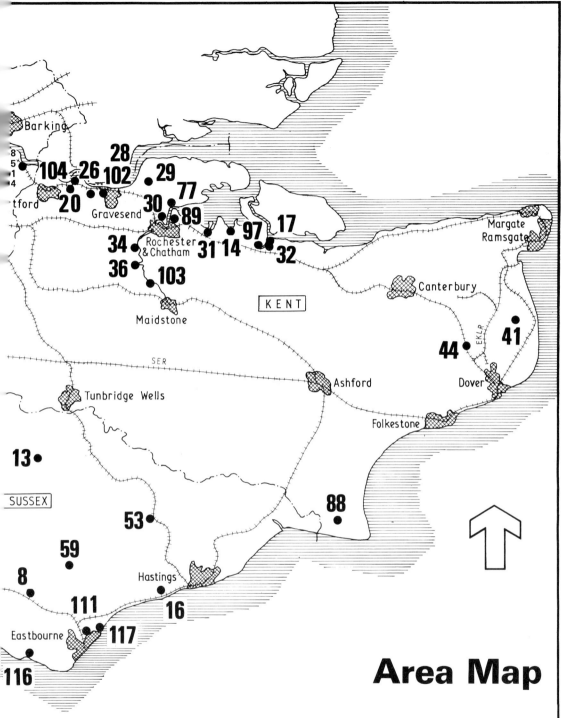

Barking

8
5
1
4

104 26 28 102 29

tford 20 Gravesend 30 77 89

34 Rochester & Chatham 31 14 97 17 32

36 103

Maidstone

KENT

Margate
Ramsgate

Canterbury

SER

Ashford

Tunbridge Wells

44 EKLR 41

Dover

Folkestone

13

SUSSEX

53

88

59

8

Hastings

111 16

Eastbourne 117

116

Area Map

Showing location of railways described

Numbers refer to photographs

(or the first number of a series)

Drawn by D.H.Smith

BRICKS & BLOCKS

1. A late survivor amongst the Sussex industrial narrow gauge was the little 2ft 0in gauge system at Thakeham Tiles, near Storrington. The original locos were all built at the works using a variety of engines mounted on Hudson skip chassis. This particular locomotive had an Armstrong Siddeley engine, and after replacement by more conventional motive power, it was sold to an enthusiast from Nottingham in 1969. (C.G. Down)

⟶

3. Another view of Hunslet 3653, pausing on the footpath bridge. Despite an enthusiastic management and staff, it was ultimately decided to replace the line with a conveyor belt. All was not lost however, for after the last train ran on 14th November 1980, the Company most generously gave the entire railway system to the nearby Chalk Pits Museum. It was removed over the following weekend and all of it has been put to good use in the industrial narrow gauge section of the Museum. (D.H. Smith)

2. The raison d'être of the Thakeham line was the movement of coloured sand within the works. The original home-made motive power was replaced in the late 1960s with four Hunslet diesels acquired second-hand from a variety of sources. One of them was used daily shuttling to and fro continuously hauling a couple of skips of sand over a short, sharply curved line. This view, taken in August 1979 shows Hunslet 3653, built in 1946 for Enfield Rolling Mills, Middlesex, on its daily duties. (D.H. Smith)

4. The North Holmwood works, near Dorking, of Redland Bricks (formerly Sussex & Dorking United Brick Cos) had a very interesting method of operating their railway. Originally horse worked, locomotives were acquired for the 2ft 0in gauge line in the early 1950s. In 1961, this BEV battery electric loco (WR 4998) was converted to driverless automatic operation. On completion of loading with clay, the operator set the train in motion, which proceeded to the works unattended until it hit a trip ramp. This loco can now be seen at the Chalk Pits Museum. (C.F. Bowles/CPM Library)

5. The auto trip ramp on the approach to a junction at North Holmwood. Here the ramp was raised or lowered according to which way the points were set, but at the end of the line, fixed ramps were provided. (C.F. Bowles/CPM Library)

6. To get the clay into the works, the loaded skips were hauled up this incline (there was a second one to another part of the works) by a stationary engine. North Holmwood works produced the well-known Dorking Red bricks until its closure in 1981. (C.F. Bowles/CPM Library)

7. To cover the possible failure of one of the auto locomotives, this small manually driven 0–4–0 battery loco (WR 4634/51) was kept at North Holmwood as spare. (C.F. Bowles/CPM Library)

8. Near Berwick station in Sussex, the Ludlay Brick & Tile Co had a 2ft 0in gauge tramway from the claypit to the works. This was originally a Motor Rail petrol loco (52XX series of 1931), but was rebuilt at Ludlay with a Perkins diesel engine and radiator from a Trojan lorry. Seen here after closure in 1966, the loco was obtained for preservation by Claude Jessett of Hadlow Down. (E.B. Benn)

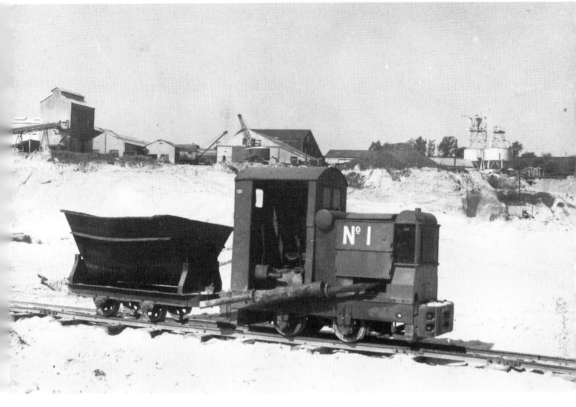

10. The mainstay of the Standard Brick fleet were a number of Ruston & Hornsby diesels. Amongst them was No. 1 (RH 191670/38) seen here with a skip built by Allens of Tipton. The formerly extensive system was entirely replaced by conveyor belts by 1964. (C.G. Down)

9. Originally built for War Department service in World War I, this 2ft 0in gauge 0–6–0WT Hudswell Clarke 1314 of 1918 later pursued a varied career with several owners in the West Country before ending its days with the Standard Brick & Sand Co at Holmthorpe, Redhill, where it was photographed by the late George Alliez in 1936. (Courtesy B.D. Stoyel)

11. As well as their standard range of geared locomotives, Sentinel also rebuilt a number of conventional industrial locomotives with their patent high pressure boiler. Such conversions are readily recognisable from the standard product as they utilised the original locomotive frames, wheels and coupling rods, but even so, it is difficult to reconcile the ugly duckling that was the Standard Brick & Sand Co's *Gervase* with what had once been a graceful Manning Wardle 0–4–0ST. (F. Jones)

12. The Standard Brick & Sand Co had another peculiar one-off Sentinel DOM (the name is taken from the Dorking, Oxted and Merstham lime works) which started life as the power unit of a Sentinel steam railcar on the ill-fated Jersey Eastern Railway. When the latter line closed, the coach part was left behind in Jersey as a summer house, and the business end rebuilt to form a useful, if somewhat unorthodox shunting locomotive. It was later rebuilt with an ugly sheet steel body that completely disguised its railcar origins. (A. Neale Collection)

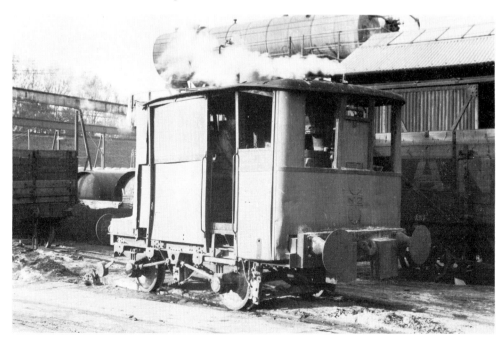

13. The 2ft 0in gauge system serving Crowborough Brickworks in Sussex was unusual in that it did not serve the clay pit (which was road worked) but transported bricks within the works itself. When the original fleet of Lister diesel locomotives became unfit for further service, they were replaced by a fleet of small BEV battery locomotives. Two of these W217 class 0–4–0 locos are seen resting between duties in August 1979, with the BR Tunbridge Wells to Uckfield line in the background. The works ceased production the following February. (D.H. Smith)

14. Few people will know that a pioneer among early electric railways was a 2ft 0in gauge brickworks line at Lower Halstow on the Medway estuary. As early as 1902, Eastwoods Ltd replaced horses with a trolley pole loco built by A. Hirst & Son of Dewsbury. Details are obscure, but the line, which connected the works with its claypit and a wharf on Halstow creek, is believed to have ceased operating in the 1920s. (C.G. Down Collection)

15. During the late 1920s, Sentinel of Shrewsbury, designed a cheap and simple narrow gauge version of their standard gauge geared steam locomotive. Apart from the usual high pressure Sentinel vertical boiler, the locomotives were designed for easy conversion from one gauge to another. The Woodside Brick Works at Croydon had two of these locos, and Sentinel 6742 is shown dumped awaiting its fate in 1953. (F. Jones)

16. A scene that could have been any one of innumerable brickworks tramways in the South East. A view down the incline at Baxters Brickworks, Bexhill, in 1962, with a Motor Rail diesel (ex petrol) loco (MR 5292 of 1931) shunting skips in the clay pit. (C.G. Down)

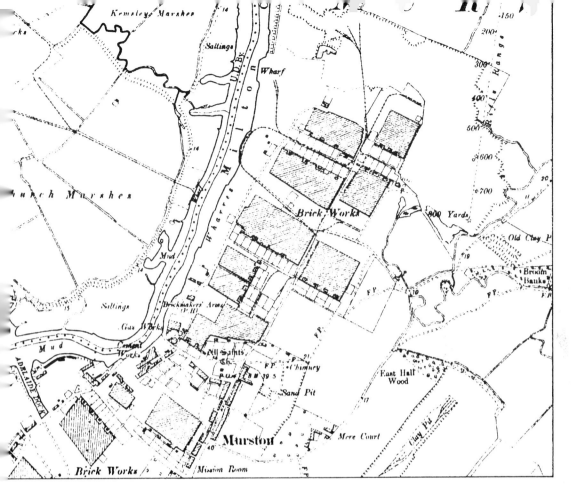

1898 map-scale 6" to the mile.

17. Early petrol locomotives often utilised an engine that might have a variety of other applications, The Meadows 4EB engine that the Kent Construction Co and their successors F.C. Hibberd fitted to the 10HP class of petrol locomotives was also used in Invicta and "chain gang" Frazer Nash sports cars, as well as in marine applications. Three of these locomotives line up at APCMs Murston Brickworks near Sittingbourne in 1963. (C.G. Down)

18. The firm of Midhurst Whites produces sand/lime bricks at their works on the outskirts of Midhurst in Sussex. At one time they possessed no less than three, unconnected, 2ft 6in gauge railways worked by a variety of petrol and diesel locomotives. All three lines remained in situ until very recent times, but the last to be used (indeed, the penultimate narrow gauge industrial line in Sussex) was that to the sandpit. Crossing over the site of the Midhurst to Petersfield branch railway en route, the end of the line, at the working face, is seen in this view taken in 1976. (D.H. Smith)

CEMENT

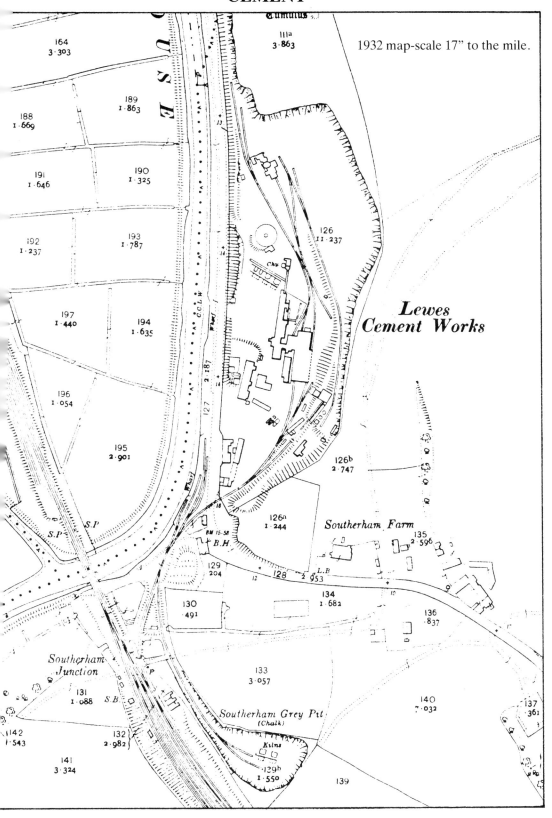

1932 map-scale 17" to the mile.

Lewes
Cement Works

Southerham Farm

Southerham
Junction

Southerham Grey Pit
(Chalk)

19. Shunting in the rain at Lewes Cement Works is Hawthorn Leslie 0–4–0ST *Atlas* No. 17 (HL 2532/02). Following replacement by a diesel it was sold for scrap in 1966, but mouldered away at the back of the works for several more years whilst its new owner vainly attempted to resell her. (Hugh Davies)

21. Showing signs of sundry makeshift repairs is Kent Work's *Clarence*. Reputedly built by the Middlesborough firm of T.D. Ridley in 1899, it was far more likely a rebuild by them of an older Barclay loco. (F. Jones)

20. The end of the line. Lying dumped in the bushes awaiting their fate at APCM's Kent Cement Works at Stone, near Dartford in 1947, are Hudswell Clarke saddletanks *Toronto* (HC 571/00 left), and *Stone* (HC 298/88 right). (F. Jones)

22. Far better known for their diesel locomotives, Brush Electrical Engineering and their predecessors, Falcon and Henry Hughes, built numerous small steam locomotives in earlier years. Typical of these was Kent Work's *Elephant* (BE 277/98) which put in many years of good service before being cut up in 1960. (F. Jones)

24. Just to the east of Kent Works was Johnson's Cement Works. Originally, this had a narrow gauge system with the peculiar gauge of 3ft 9½in. Replaced by standard gauge in 1928, Bagnall 0–4–0ST *Leviathan* and the nameless Aveling geared locomotive still survived, but out of use, when this photograph was taken on 2nd July 1932. (G. Alliez, courtesy B.D. Stoyel)

←————————

23. The Kent Work's locomotive fleet also included a pair of Manning Wardle 0–6–0STs. *Apex* was a victim of the 1960 scrap drive, but *Arthur* (MW 1601/03), seen here with the works in the background, was more lucky and remained in use until 1967 before going to the Kent & East Sussex Railway for preservation. (C.G. Down)

25. Four coupled Peckett saddletanks predominated in the replacement standard gauge fleet at Johnson's Works. Most were built new, but *New Globe* was a transfer from the nearby Globe Cement Works, which ceased production around this time. (F. Jones)

27. The replacement standard gauge system at Swanscombe was worked by a fleet of Hawthorn Leslie 0–4–0STs. No. 5 (HL 3719/29) shunts the exchange sidings at the beginning of the 1½ mile line down to the chalk pits. (A. Neale Collection)

26. The narrow gauge (3ft 5½in) system at Swanscombe was surely unique in the UK in having locomotives and stock with *outside* flanged wheels. In keeping with this eccentricity was the weird and wonderful locomotive fleet which included a vertical boilered DeWinton, a well tank by Stephen Lewin, several Aveling & Porter geared locos, and four Wilkinson steam tram locos acquired from the Plymouth & Devonport Tramways in 1905. Compared with this lot, *Hustler,* one of a batch of 0–4–0ST s by the obscure Kilmarnock Engineering Co, seemed positively commonplace!
(Ken Nunn, courtesy LCGB)

28. At APCM's Bevan's Works in Northfleet, a short 2ft 0in gauge line operated on a riverside wharf. Ruston & Hornsby diesel 181824 is seen with a background of shipping on 3rd September 1962. (C.G. Down)

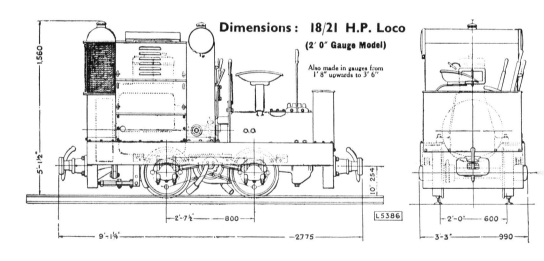

Dimensions : 18/21 H.P. Loco
(2' 0" Gauge Model)

Also made in gauges from
1' 8" upwards to 3' 6"

1,560

5'-1½"

2'-7½" — 800

10" 254

L5386

9'-1¼" — 2775

2'-0" — 600

3'-3" — 990

30. At Frindsbury, on the River Medway opposite Rochester, an amalgamation of seven small works produced the Crown & Quarry Works of APCM. In this view, *George,* a standard gauge Peckett 0–4–0ST (759/99) stands at the quarry face on 2nd December 1951, while its train of ancient tipping wagons is loaded by the navvies; the one on the upper ledge being steam driven. *George* was scrapped in 1960, and the works closed in 1963. (J.H. Meredith)

29. The Alpha Cement Co works at Cliffe-at-Hoo had a 2ft 0in gauge railway operated largely by a fleet of Ruston diesels. Three second-hand John Fowler diesels were also acquired, this is *Layer* (JF 21294/36), but sister loco *Peldon* is now preserved at the Chalk Pits Museum. In this view, taken on 19th April 1958, a load of chalk is about to be tipped onto the conveyor belt below. (S.A. Leleux)

31. Although a number of 2ft 0in gauge Baldwins from World War I were sold to public narrow gauge lines in Britain, only one went into industry. Here, no 45142 lies derelict at the British Standard Cement Works at Rainham, following closure of the works in 1932.
(G. Alliez, courtesy B.D. Stoyel)

32. The last surviving narrow gauge steam loco in the cement industry was the 4ft 3in gauge Barclay 0–4–0ST *Wouldham* at APCM's Sittingbourne Works. Cut up in 1960, one of her works plates survives in the Chalk Pits Museum collection. (F. Jones)

33. Following *Wouldham's* withdrawal, the lengthy tramway across the fields from the claypits at Murston to the works was worked by two small Hibberd "Planet" diesels. This scene at the claypits was taken in September 1964, and Bowater's paper mills at Kemsley can be seen in the background. (C.G. Down)

34. Until 1952, the RPCM cement works at Halling included an extensive 2ft 0in gauge system. A German built Orenstein & Koppel diesel shunts a train of skips. (J.H. Meredith)

35. Clay for APCM's Holborough cement works was supplied from a nearby pit at Paddlesworth, which had a 3ft 0in gauge railway worked by seven Ruston & Hornsby diesels. Works and claypit were connected by an aerial ropeway, the Paddlesworth terminus being this shed, in which the ropeway buckets were transferred to flat wagons. (C.G. Down)

36. APCM Holborough had the last Aveling & Porter traction-engine-on-rails built in 1926. Although obsolete by the time it was built, this loco survived to be donated in 1964 to the Bluebell Railway for preservation. (F. Jones)

37. Until replacement by standard gauge in 1954, Holborough Works also used a 3ft 0in gauge railway in the chalk pit. Ruston diesel no. 200524 is seen hauling a heavy train of 18 loaded skips from the pit on 8th April 1950. Note the steam navvy in the distance. (J.H. Meredith)

38. Transatlantic import. The 3ft 0in gauge Montreal 0–4–0ST lying derelict at Holborough in 1949. (F. Jones)

39. Typifying Bagnall's standard designs of narrow gauge 0–4–0ST, WB 2073 of 1918 is seen in 1935 on the 2ft 0in gauge tramway which ran from Holborough Cement Works to wharves on the River Medway. The main line from Strood to Maidstone West, which still serves the works, can be seen in the background. (G. Alliez, courtesy B.D. Stoyel)

40. *Charlton* (S.8796/33) was one of several 100hp double geared Sentinel steam locomotives supplied to William Cory & Son Ltd's large coal wharf on the Thames at Gallions, East London. In 1950, they were moved down stream for a few more years work at the same firms Rochester wharf before being displaced by diesels and scrapped in 1956. (A. Neale Collection)

41. The only coal in the South East was found deep underground in the area between Dover and Deal in Kent. Betteshanger Colliery took delivery of No. 9, an "Austerity" 0–6–0ST, in 1954 (Hunslet Engine Co works no. 3825) and it was later transferred to Snowdown Colliery. (F. Jones)

42. Another Hunslet Austerity 0–6–0ST at Betteshanger was No. 10 (HE 3827/54). These locomotives were built in large numbers by several manufacturers from World War II onwards and became the mainstay of numerous collieries throughout the country. (F. Jones)

44. *St Dunstan* was transferred to Snowdown in the 1950s, and is seen there shunting internal user (hence the X) coal wagons. (CPM Library)

3. Pearson & Dorman Long Ltd, who owned Betteshanger Colliery before the advent of the NCB, named several of their locomotives after local Saints. *St Dunstan* was a powerful 0–6–0 saddletank built by the Avonside Engine Co (works no 2004) in 1927. (F. Jones)

CONTRACTORS

45. In the 1920s and 1930s, the London County Council built a large housing estate between Wimbledon and Sutton, known as St Helier. The main contractors, C.J. Wills & Sons Ltd, utilised a standard gauge light railway running from sidings at Mitcham on the Croydon to Wimbledon line of the Southern Railway. The fleet of locomotives consisted largely of Manning Wardle six coupled saddletanks; this is *Mermaid* (MW 1294/84) on 7th August 1935.
(G. Alliez, courtesy B.D. Stoyel)

47. It is interesting to note that three of the most prolific builders of contractors locos were neighbours in Jack Lane, Leeds. As well as Manning Wardle, there was the Hunslet Engine Co and Hudswell Clarke; one of the latter's products, no 440 of 1896, *Barry*, was typical, and had a well travelled life with several owners. This picture was taken in 1937 during the construction of the Southern Railway's Chessington branch, a line which, but for World War II, would have run through to Leatherhead.
(D.H. Smith Collection)

46. Two of C.J. Wills locomotives at St Helier were amongst the last produced by Manning Wardle; *Edgware* and *Hendon* had previously been used on contracts to extend the London Underground to these two places. *Hendon* (MW 2046/26) is seen with the crew posing proudly by their charge in 1933. (D.H. Smith Collection)

48. Sir Robert McAlpine & Sons almost exclusively favoured Hudswell Clarke for their large fleet of steam locomotives. Amongst them were a number of Hudswell standard designs of 0–6–0ST with 12in x 18in inside cylinders. McAlpine's No. 33 (HC 1029/13) was photographed on a contract at Worcester Park, Surrey, in 1936. (G. Alliez, courtesy B.D. Stoyel)

50. Amongst the more unusual locomotives on the Sutton contract were a batch of these Hudswell 0–6–0Ts. Built new as 3ft 6in gauge in 1925 for McAlpine's Sekondi Harbour construction contract in the Gold Coast, they were designed for easy conversion to 3ft 0in gauge, and on completion of the contract were shipped back to England for use on the South Merton to Sutton job.
(F. Jones Collection)

49. Amongst the last major contracts in the area to use the traditional fleet of 3ft 0in and standard gauge steam locos was McAlpine's contract for the South Merton to Sutton section of the Southern Railway. The contract involved very considerable earthworks, and at one time an injunction was received from local residents complaining of the noise made by working 24 hours a day.

3ft 0in gauge no. 12 (HC 1037/13) rests between duties at Sutton in the summer of 1929. (R.A. Wheeler)

51. Between the wars, Surrey County Council had a large fleet of 2ft 0in gauge steam and petrol locomotives for use on their various road construction schemes. GP40 was one of a pair of Hudswell Clarke 0–6–0WTs (HC 1645/30) employed on the Guildford By-pass contract. Here it is seen in use on the Hogs Back on 13th May 1931. Note the substantial bars, fore and aft of the wheels, to prevent damage in the event of a derailment. Its sister engine, GP39 (HC 1643/30) still survives at the Bressingham Steam Museum in Norfolk, after a long period of service at the Penrhyn Slate Quarries in North Wales. (G. Alliez, courtesy B.D. Stoyel)

52. A scene that completely typifies the Victorian railway construction period. A pair of Manning Wardle K class 0–6–0STs, each with its train of wooden side tippers on a contract at Guildford in 1890. Lucas & Aird were one of the principal railway contractors, and built the Direct Line through Cobham to Guildford in 1882–4, but the nature of their 1890 contract at Guildford and the precise identity of the two Mannings illustrated here, are still a matter of debate amongst industrial railway historians. (F. Jones Collection)

GYPSUM

53. The standard Bagnall 0–4–0ST with 14 inch diameter outside cylinders was a well made if not particularly beautiful machine that enjoyed a good reputation with industrial locomotive operators. *Sirapite* No. 2 (WB 2369/28) put in nearly forty years service with Gypsum Mines Ltd, at Mountfield, Sussex, before all three steam locomotives here were cut up on for scrap in 1967. (CPM Library)

54. Another Mountfield locomotive was *Kemp*, a powerful Barclay 0–6–0ST (AB 2241/48) seen here shunting wagons of coal for the works in the 1950s. Gypsum is the principal constituent of plaster and plaster boards. (D.H. Smith Collection)

55. The Sub-Wealden Gypsum Co Ltd was formed in 1876, the presence of gypsum deep underground at Mountfield having been discovered four years earlier. A mile long standard gauge connection was laid in, and the first locomotive acquired at the same time. It is interesting to note that the first two chairmen of the company were Messrs Hook and Baxter of the Dorking Greystone Lime Co whose names were given to locomotives there, see photographs 63 and 70. This aerial view of what was by then the Mountfield works of Gypsum Mines Ltd was taken in the mid-1950s. (CPM Library)

56. In 1945 this inclined adit (also seen in the foreground of photograph 55) was driven to replace the previously used vertical shafts. 2ft 0in gauge tracks were laid worked by moving cables on the incline and battery electric locomotives underground. This photograph was also taken in the mid-1950s. (CPM Library)

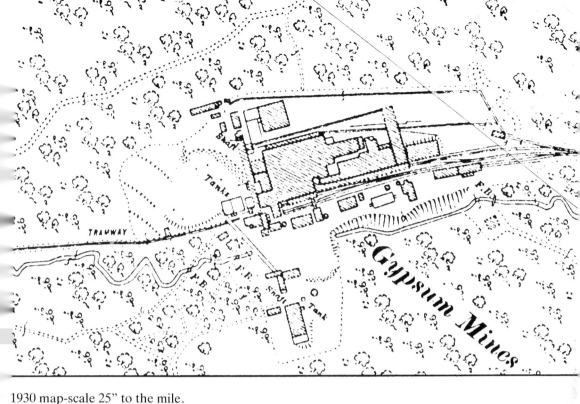

1930 map-scale 25" to the mile.

57. Mountfield gypsum mines are still a major source of traffic onto the Tonbridge to Hastings railway, but nowadays internal traffic is worked by a pair of Thomas Hill "Vanguard" diesel hydraulic locomotives. This view shows no. 1 (TH 183V/67) when almost new. (CPM Library)

58. Rail traffic has now ceased at British Gypsum's Erith works, and *Princess Margaret* is out of use. Built as Barclay 376 in 1948 for Lever Bros at Port Sunlight, it also put in a spell of duty at the neighbouring BOCM oil cake works (see photo 94) before coming to British Gypsum in 1971. (A. Neale Collection)

HOSPITAL

59. Most of the large mental hospitals built in the late Victorian and the Edwardian eras were provided with a rail connection, primarily for the delivery of coal for the hospital boilers, but also for the conveyance of staff, patients and visitors, where the distance from the nearest main line station was great enough. Like several similar systems, the Hellingly Hospital railway in Sussex was electrified on the overhead wire principle and the single locomotive was built by William Whiteley & Sons of Huddersfield. The line closed in March 1959 after conversion of the hospital boilers to oil firing, and although regular passenger services had not been operated since 1931, occasional enthusiast specials were run, such as this one. (P. Hay)

1932 map-scale 6" to the mile.

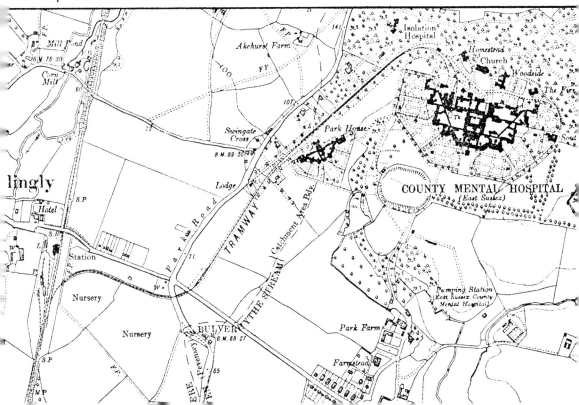

60. The Brockham Lime & Hearthstone Co limeworks was probably best known for later providing the home for the Brockham Museum. However, this view is of interest for showing both horse haulage and cable haulage of standard gauge wagons in the 1920s when the works was already semi-derelict. It closed in 1936. Although it never possessed any locomotives, the site had a fascinating history starting with the Brockham Brick Co in the 1870s, through bankruptcy and auction in 1910 when the BL&HCo was formed. In a small area, sand, bricks, hearthstone and lime were produced, as the maps show. (CPM Library)

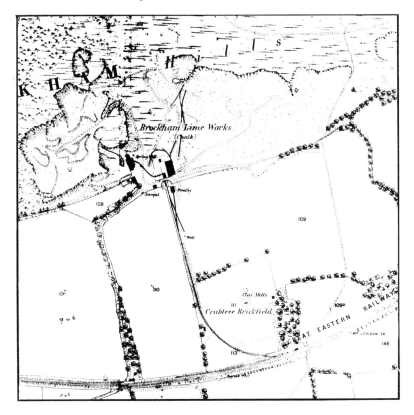

1882

896   1914

Brockham Lime and Hearthstone Company Ltd.

Secretary:
HAROLD EVANS, F.C.A.

Telephone:
BETCHWORTH 3317.

Registered Office:
THE LIME WORKS
BETCHWORTH
SURREY

Works:
BROCKHAM SIDING, S.R.
(NR. BETCHWORTH)

61. Amongst the traditional steam locomotive builders, John Fowler of Leeds pioneered the development of internal combustion locos, building their first petrol loco in 1923. Fowler 17726 was a four coupled petrol locomotive built in 1929, and after a replacement diesel engine had been fitted, it spent the last fifteen years of its life at Hall & Co's Coulsdon Limeworks. Note that Fowler, like many other steam builders fitted a traditiona chimney to many of their IC locos – a con venient and attractive means of dispersing exhaust fumes. (K. Broderick)

62. The Oxted Greystone Lime Co once had a lengthy standard gauge siding connection and a 2ft 0in gauge network. By the 1950s, only a 50 yard section of 2ft 0in gauge was left to convey chalk to the kilns. As a locomotive needed repairs, it was replaced by one from another works; thus at one time it possessed one wagon but four locos! The tiny system closed in 1971. (E. Jackson Collection)

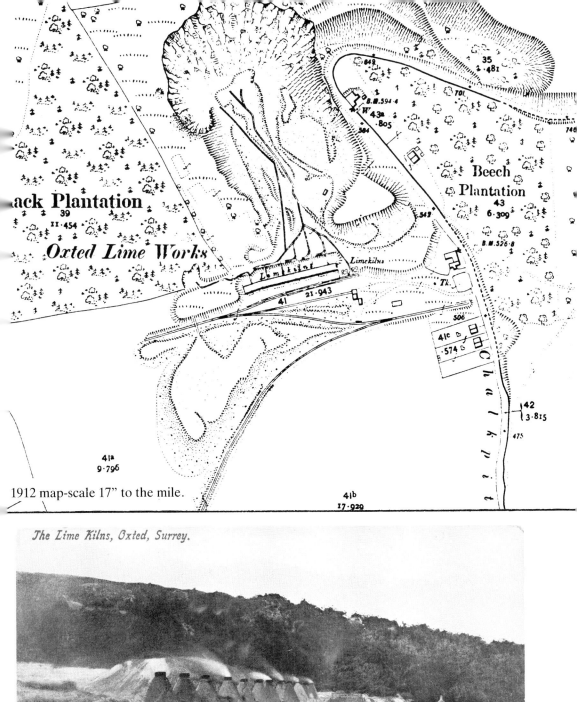

ack Plantation
39
II·454

Oxted Lime Works

Beech
Plantation
43
6·309

Limekilns

1912 map-scale 17" to the mile.

41a
9·796

41b
17·929

The Lime Kilns, Oxted, Surrey.

63. The Dorking Greystone Lime Co at Betchworth was well known to enthusiasts even in the 1930s, and photographic coverage is thus very good. The works is of particular interest to the Chalk Pits Museum, because it was the acquisition of this locomotive, *Townsend Hook*, built by Fletcher Jennings in 1880, which started the Brockham Museum collection. The gauge is the very unusual 3ft 2¼in, and the picture was taken in 1949. (E.C. Griffith/Lens of Sutton)

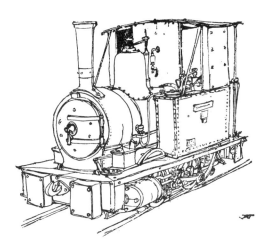

65. A notable feature of the 3ft 2¼in network was the main incline on which wagons were hauled up by a loco running on a lesser incline, connected by a rope completing the third side of a "triangle". *William Finlay* is seen at the foot of the incline (with the rope behind it) in August 1953, a year before closure of the 3ft 2¼in lines. (P. Hay)

64. Sister locomotive *William Finlay* was originally identical, but here shows certain differences, notably the safety valves. The names of the twins were applied in 1930 by the publicity conscious Managing Director Major E.W. Taylerson, after company chairmen; previously they had been simply numbers 4 and 5. The loco was acquired for preservation by Mr J.B. Latham, who has recently placed it on loan to the Chalk Pits Museum. (F. Jones)

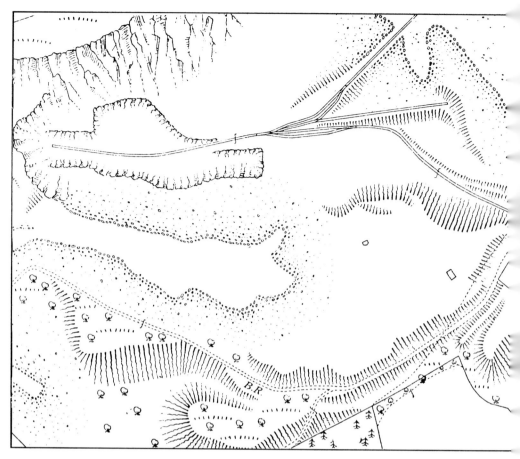

66. The wagons were of an archaic design, both side- and end-tipping, although one man could easily tip the load into the kilns. This view was taken after the railway closed and shows wagons pushed over by vandals; in service only the body would have been tipped. (P. Myatt)

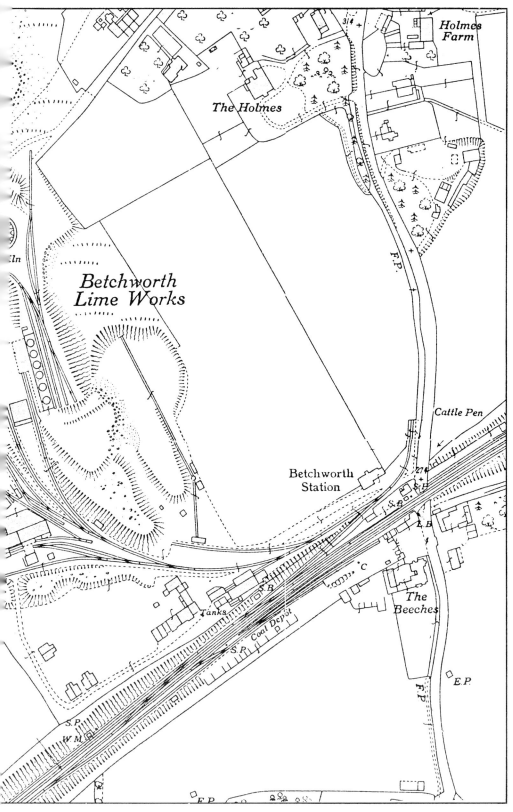

1930 map-scale 25" to the mile.

67. In 1945 an Orenstein & Koppel "Montannia" diesel was obtained for the 3ft 2¼in lines. Nicknamed *Monty* by the staff, it was the last loco to be used on that gauge, and can now be seen at the Chalk Pits Museum. (P. Myatt)

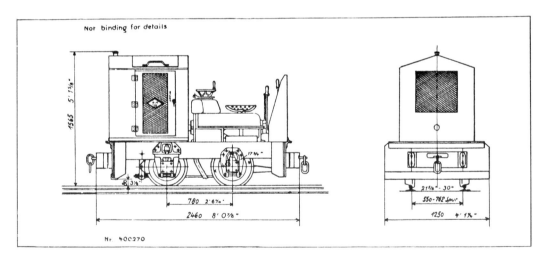

69. The standard gauge sidings at Betchworth were worked by three steam locomotives; this was the first, a vertical boilered geared machine by T.H. Head of Middlesborough. After construction of a hydrator plant in 1924, 2ft 0in gauge skips were conveyed by transporter wagons between the kilns and the plant. Thus there were two unconnected 2ft 0in gauge non-locomotive worked lines at low level, as well as the third unconnected loco worked line (see photo 68). A third narrow gauge, 1ft 7in, operated in the hearthstone mines. (E.C. Griffith/Lens of Sutton)

68. Another O & K diesel was bought in 1952, but this time of 2ft 0in gauge, and it was set to work in one of the upper chalk pits. After closure of all the railways, it was brought down to the lime kilns, as seen here, and subsequently donated to Brockham Museum. It can now, of course, be seen at Chalk Pits; thus all the narrow gauge locos from Betchworth are at one location again. (C.G. Down)

70. The third standard gauge steam locomotive at Betchworth (the second having been disposed of as early as 1878) was *Baxter* (or *Captain Baxter*). Built by Fletcher Jennings in 1877, it was, in effect, an enlarged version of the 3ft 2¼in gauge pair, and is seen here shunting wagons by the eastern battery of lime kilns on 6th September 1958. This locomotive is now preserved on the Bluebell Railway. (P. Myatt)

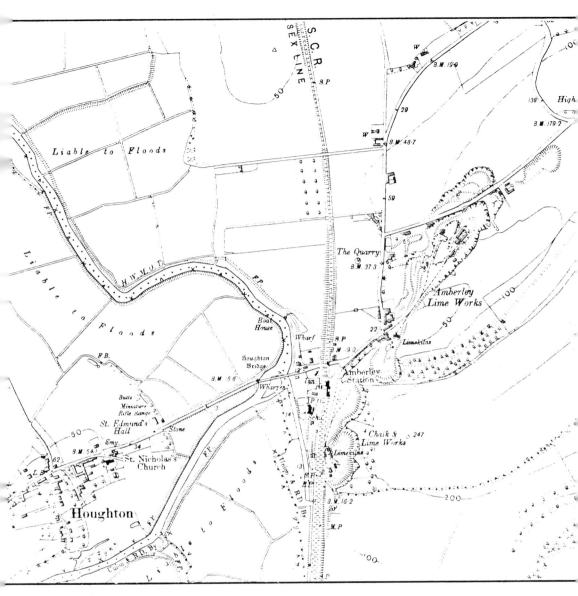

1914 map-scale 6" to the mile.

71. Also of special interest to the Chalk Pits was Pepper & Co at Amberley in Sussex, since the Museum now occupies the site. A network of standard gauge tracks was operated; very little is known about the first steam locomotive, but the second was this 0–4–0 geared machine built by Marshall of Gainsborough in 1878. It is basically an under-running (cylinders beneath the boiler) traction engine mounted on railway wheels, but was unfortunately scrapped in 1959. (F. Jones)

72. Peppers third locomotive was another traction-engine-on-rails, this time by Aveling & Porter of Rochester (AP 4371/99). Note the extra belt drive wheel, mounted on the flywheel, for driving flint crushing machinery near the loco shed, and also the apparent coupling rod, which in fact couples the wheel centres; coupling was actually accomplished by internal gearing. Like the Marshall, this loco was scrapped in 1958. The building in the background of this photo (and no. 71) now houses the Museum's introductory slide show. (F. Jones)

74. The main bank of lime kilns at Peppers works was built about 1905 to a Belgian design. Both the Marshall and the Aveling can be seen by the DeWit kilns soon after construction; note the typical wagons used for transporting finished lime products with tarpaulins lettered Pepper & Co. Much altered, these kilns still exist as part of the Museum. (CPM Library)

73. In 1953, Pepper & Co obtained this small four wheeled diesel from F.C. Hibberd (FH 3643). It displaced the two steam locos, but did not last very long, for the works closed and the entire railway was scrapped around 1962. (C.G. Down)

LOAM

75. For over one hundred years until 1957, loam for metal casting moulds was transported from the pits to the Thames quayside by J. Parish & Co at Erith, on the 4ft 0in gauge. Several locomotives were used, the last being no IV built by Hawthorn Leslie in 1903 (HL 2565). (J. Meredith)

76. The railway crossed West Street, Erith on the level, in parallel with the standard gauge line of Messrs Fraser. At one time Erith Council tram tracks crossed the railway here, but by the time this picture was taken on 16th June 1950, trams had been replaced by trolleybuses. (J. Meredith)

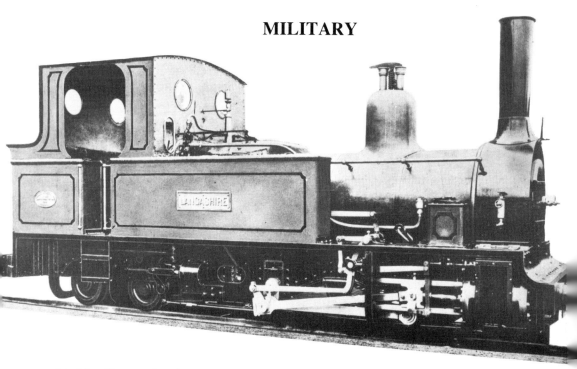

77. The Chattenden & Upnor Railway has been mentioned briefly in the Introduction. It was a 2ft 6in gauge line running from a pontoon wharf on the River Medway, near the attractive hamlet of Upnor, to Chattenden and Lodge Hill depots. Among the early locomotives supplied was *Lancashire*, an 0–4–4T built by the Yorkshire Engine Co in 1891, and scrapped in 1932.
(F. Jones Collection)

79. Another 0–4–2T was built by Peckett & Co (no. 1868) a year later in 1934, and named *Norbury*. As can be seen this had much larger tanks, but was built to the same specification. The nameplate and worksplate of *Norbury* are also preserved at the Chalk Pits Museum. (F. Jones)

78. In the 1930s, the Admiralty, who had taken over from the Royal Engineers after they had moved to Longmoor, ordered some 0–4–2 tank locomotives from different manufacturers for comparison trials. This is *Burnett Hall*, built by the Avonside Engine Co (no. 2070) in 1933. The nameplate from this loco is now preserved at the Chalk Pits Museum. (F. Jones)

80. After World War II this 0–6–0 diesel mechanical was purchased from Baguley-Drewry (DC 2263/49), which is seen coupled to the line's Wickham built combination coach on a pleasantly wooded section of the line. Both vehicles are still in existence on the Welshpool & Llanfair Railway. (S.A. Leleux)

82. The twin level crossings by St Phillip & St James church, looking for all the world like main line ones, were controlled by the Church Crossing junction signal box and protected by full signalling. The line in the foreground ran down to the pontoon wharf, and the branch, by then disused, ran to Lower Upnor. 8th April 1950. (J.H. Meredith)

81. Chattenden depot yard on 8th April 1950. Visible in the middle distance is one of the toastrack coaches, and on the left, one of the numerous battery-electric locos no. 89, built by Greenwood & Batley (GB 1984/45). (J.H. Meredith)

83. Although seldom visited by enthusiasts, the railways of the Royal Arsenal at Woolwich were probably the most extensive in the area. Covering 1,300 acres, the first section of 1ft 6in gauge track was opened in 1873 and by the 1920s when these photographs were taken, 118 standard and narrow gauge locomotives were at work. This is *Hannibal* built by Hudswell Clarke (works no 281) in 1885. (CPM Library)

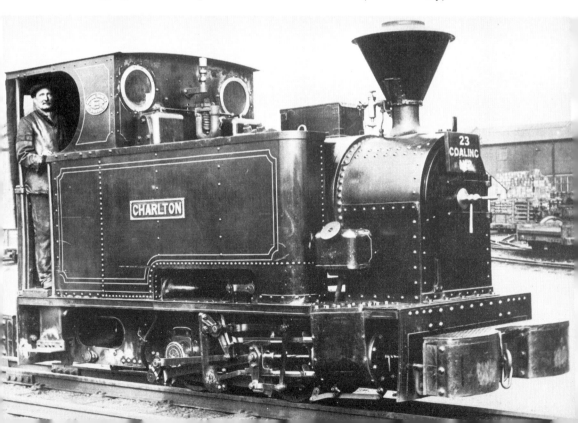

85. McEwan Pratt & Co Ltd of Wickford in Essex, was one of the pioneers of commercial IC locomotives. *Megaera* was a four-wheel petrol locomotive built in 1914. Amongst the features was the centre cab with radiating cooling pipes at each end, the long overall roof, and the outside drive chains. *Megaera* was sold to the Lewes cement works where it survived until about 1930. (CPM Library)

84. *Charlton* was an 0–4–0T built by the Avonside Engine Co (works no. 1752) in 1916. Note the spark arrester chimney (essential with all that ammunition about!). A similar locomotive, *Woolwich*, now operates on the Bicton Woodland Railway in Devon. In true military tradition, the loco carries a headboard indicating the duties it was engaged on. (CPM Library)

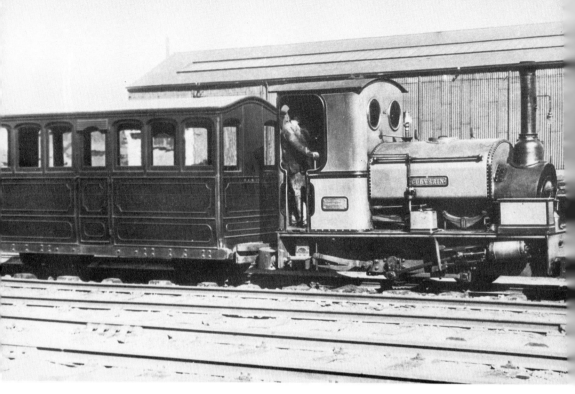

86. Extensive passenger services were provided for the workmen at Woolwich Arsenal, both first and second classes! Here, *Culverin,* the second Hudswell Clarke 0–4–0ST supplied (HC 269 of 1884) is coupled to a first class saloon coach. The peculiar shape at the base of the chimney is a type of spark arrester fitted to many of the locomotives. (CPM Library)

88. Not far from Dungeness and the Romney Hythe & Dymchurch Railway are the extensive weapon ranges at Lydd. A network of 2ft 0in gauge tracks operates throughout the ranges, used mainly by target trolleys but among the few locomotives is Ruston & Hornsby 202000 of 1940, here coupled to a pair of bogie vehicles. (M.P. Hayter)

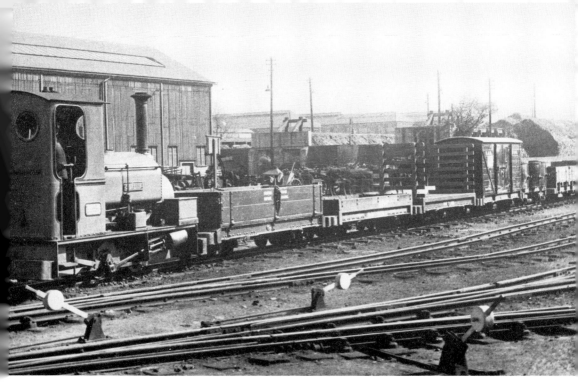

87. *Culverin* again, shunting a selection of goods stock, some of which now survives on the Bicton Woodland Railway, while a gunpowder van can be seen at the Conway Valley Railway Museum at Bettws-y-Coed. (CPM Library)

89. In the news recently because of its closure was the Chatham Naval Dockyard. Right up to the end, a standard gauge steam locomotive, *Ajax,* was kept in working order as a standby. Here can be seen an earlier view of another Hawthorn 0–4–0ST, *Sussex,* (HL 2876/11), with the vessel "Fort Dunvegan" forming the backdrop. (F. Jones)

90. The Royal Aircraft Establishment at Farnborough is still well known for its annual Air Show, but until 1968 a standard gauge railway, laid largely in the road, tramway fashion, ran from Farnborough Station (LSWR). Locomotive No. 7, carrying a plate reading ROF No. 5 (Royal Ordnance Factory), built by Hudswell Clarke in 1941 (works no. 1723) leaves the tramway on the approach to the station. (A. Neale Collection)

MISCELLANEOUS MANUFACTURING

91. British Insulated Callender's Cables Ltd used a 3ft 6in gauge railway at their cable works at Belvedere, near Erith, in that part of Kent which is now part of Greater London. The steam locomotives were converted to run on oil fuel and this view of *Woto* (Bagnall 2133 of 1924) of the seldom photographed left hand side clearly shows the rather ugly oil tank. (F. Jones)

92. BICC had three standard Bagnall 0–4–0 saddletanks. The first, named *The Mighty Atom* (!), had 6in diameter cylinders, but *Woto* seen here on 18th August 1951, had the rarer 7in cylinders. A similar loco, named *Peter* is currently awaiting restoration at the Chalk Pits Museum. (J.H. Meredith)

93. The other 7in Bagnall at BICC Belvedere was *Sir Tom* (WB 2135) which had cost £1127 when purchased new in 1925. Both *Woto* and *Sir Tom* worked until 1968 when the railway closed, having outlasted by several years the two Ruston diesels! The former were acquired for preservation and are now stored in Romford. (F. Jones)

94. Close to BICC was the works of the British Oil & Cake Mills Ltd, a subsidiary of soap manufacturers Unilever. In this line up of standard gauge locomotives can be seen Aveling & Porter 0–4–0s *Sydenham* (AP 3567 of 1895) and *Sir Vincent* (AP 8800 of 1917), with four wheel diesel *Crabtree* (RH 338416/53). *Sydenham* is now preserved at Quainton Road, while *Sir Vincent* can be seen running at the Hollycombe Steam Collection at Liphook, on summer Sundays. (Hugh Davies)

95. The well known Reading biscuit manufacturers, Huntley & Palmer, had an extensive standard gauge system until December 1969. Latterly, traffic was worked by a pair of Bagnall 0–4–0 fireless locomotives; steam, supplied by the factory "mains", being stored in hot water in the "boiler", pressure alone keeping the water on the boil. This is No. 1 (WB 2473/32), which was subsequently acquired for preservation. (A. Neale Collection)

96. The St Helens (Lancashire) firm of E. Borrows & Sons built a distinctive design of 0–4–0 well tank, supplied largely to the local glass industry. Well away from this traditional area was the Charlton works, London, of United Glass Bottle Manufacturers Ltd, where *The King,* built in 1906, was photographed. (F. Jones)

PAPER

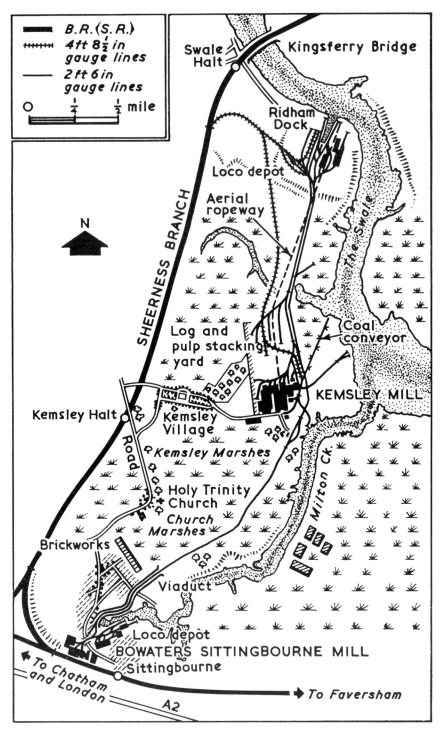

(Railway Magazine).

97. The best known narrow gauge industrial line in our area was at Bowater's Paper Mills in Sittingbourne. This 2ft 6in gauge line became the last steam worked narrow gauge industrial line in the British Isles in 1969.

However, the first steam locomotive owned by what was then, in 1905, Edward Lloyd Ltd was *Premier*, a Kerr Stuart Brazil class 0–4–2ST (works no. 886), seen here in the 1960s. (A. Muckley)

98. *Chevalier* was obtained second hand by Bowater from the Chattenden & Upnor Railway in 1950. An 0–6–2T built by Manning

Wardle in 1915 (works no. 1877), *Chevalier* is now to be seen in captivity at Whipsnade Zoo. (F. Jones)

99. Inevitably, Bowater owned some fireless steam locomotives (sparks being an obvious hazard in the paper industry). This is *Victor* built by W.G. Bagnall in 1929. The railway was used for conveying wood pulp and other supplies from wharves to the paper mill. Later the line was extended to several miles in length, connecting the new Kemsley mill and Ridham Dock with the original mill in Sittingbourne. (A. Muckley)

100. Much of the Bowaters 2ft 6in gauge railway was taken over by the Locomotive Club of Great Britain, as the Sittingbourne & Kemsley Light Railway. However, the section shown here was closed in 1969. 0–6–2T *Alpha*, built by Bagnall in 1932 (WB 2472), is seen leaving Ridham dock on 15th October 1968. (J.H. Meredith)

101. For shunting the standard gauge lines at Ridham Dock, Bowaters used 0–6–0T *Pioneer II* which had originally been SECR P class no. 178 of 1910. Note the narrow gauge level crossing. This loco has since been acquired for preservation by the Bluebell Railway. (A. Neale Collection)

102. Bowaters also operated a standard gauge railway at their works at Northfleet. Here is 0–4–0 fireless no. 1, built by Andrew Barclay (no. 1876) in 1925. (F. Jones)

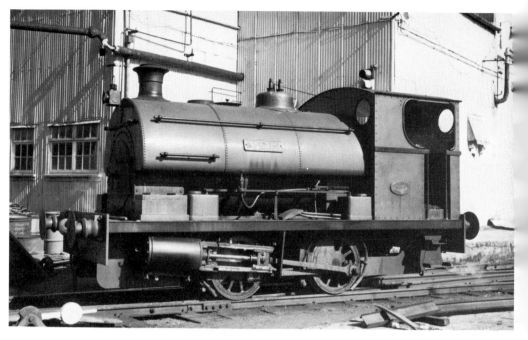

103. The other major paper manufacturing business in Kent is Reed Paper & Board (UK) Ltd. At their Aylesford Paper Mills on the River Medway near Maidstone, was *Anson*, a standard gauge Peckett 0–4–0ST (no. 2117). (F. Jones)

104. Also owned by the Reed group is the Empire Paper Mills at Greenhithe on the Thames estuary. Here, another Peckett 0–4–0ST, *Nelson* (P 1880/35), stands on the pier on 3rd September 1962. (C.G. Down)

105. In London's Old Kent Road, the South Metropolitan Gas Co, later part of the South Eastern Gas Board, operated a 3ft 0in gauge railway around the works. Two attractive 2–4–0 tank locomotives were supplied by W.G. Bagnall, the first in 1892 being named *Concord* (works no. 1421). Two very similar locomotives were used on the Rye & Camber Tramway in Sussex. (J.H. Meredith)

106. The second Bagnall delivered to the Old Kent Road gasworks was *Unity* (WB 1534) in 1898. The picture was taken on 5th May 1951 almost exactly two years before closure of the railway in May 1953. For a further two years, the pair remained on site whilst their owners tried to interest someone in preserving them. Only a nominal sum was being asked, but sadly they were cut up for scrap in 1955. (J.H. Meredith)

108. Times were hard for steam locomotive builders in the 1920s; Peckett managed to undercut Bagnalls price for repairing Vauxhall's *Orion,* and then capped that by building a close copy in 1929. This was named *Vulcan* (P 1805/29) and is seen here showing only detailed differences. Peckett went on to use a picture of *Vulcan* as the Ant class locomotive in their catalogue, but no further orders were received. (F. Jones)

107. Another South Metropolitan Gas Co works in London, at Vauxhall, had a 3ft 0in gauge railway, also using locomotives built by Bagnall, but of a rather different design. This is the third of a trio, *Orion* (WB 1536 of 1898), and is an 0–4–0 with inside cylinders and "wing" tanks either side of the smokebox. Bagnall often used inverted saddle tanks, outwardly similar, but the wing tank principle was not so common. (F. Jones)

Willingdon   Levels

F.B.

F.B.

B.M.8.3

Willingdon   Sewer

F.B.

Munl. Boro. Ry.

Lottbridge   Drove

Stone
Lott Bridge
B.M.9.3

F.P.

illingdon   Level

St.

F.B.

B.M.8.5

F.B.

F.B.

B.M.7.4

F.B.

F.B.

Queen Alexandra's
Cottage Homes

B.M.11.0

B.M.8.3

B.M.8.4

Brick
Field

M.P London 62

B.M.13.4

Horsey
B.M.31.8

B.M.85
F.B.

B.M.28.8.3

B.M.13.5

St. Andrew's Ch.
Parsonage

Schools

Laundry

Refuse Destructor Works
and Air Compressing
Station. 31

Motor Omnibus
Depot

B.M.17.5

F.P.

Ventilators

F.P.   Bea.
Farm

Nursery

ROSE LANDS P.H.

11.3

13.5

Ejector Pumping Station
(Sewage)

Southbourne   Level

F.B.

Rowlands
Terrace

11.0

Crumbles
Pond

Mission Room

Laundry

Wesley
Hall

12.0

Ch. Chap.

St. Philip's
Ch.

Sch.

Sch.   Chap.

B.M.11.8

Recreation
Ground

Lifeboat Ho.

P.H. Rocket
Ho.
Inst.

Stormwate.
Outfall

1911 map-scale 6" to the mile showing the main line to Eastbourne in the bottom left hand corner, the gasworks in the centre of the left page and the line continuing onto the shingle of the Crumbles on this page. Eastbourne Gasworks is shown in picture 111 and the later narrow gauge line on the Crumbles is illustrated in picture 117.

109. In 1902, the Croydon Gas & Coke Co took delivery of Aveling & Porter no. 4780 at their Waddon Marsh Gas Works. At one time named *Allen Lambert,* it is seen here derelict in 1960, by then owned by the South Eastern Gas Board; Waddon Marsh Halt signal box and part of Croydon Power Station can be seen in the background. (A. Neale Collection)

110. On the northern outskirts of Portsmouth is the Hilsea Gas Works, which still sees limited rail traffic. The first steam locomotive was this Beyer Peacock 0–4–0 saddletank (works no. 4664) named *Sir John Baker,* which was cut up for scrap in 1963. (A. Neale Collection)

111. The Eastbourne Gas Works of the South Eastern Gas Board acquired these two locomotives from Sydenham Gas Works around 1960. Rail Traffic ceased in 1967, and they were cut up in 1968. On the left is *Anne* (Avonside 1648 of 1914) and behind is *Mary* (Avonside 1564 of 1909) on 11th April 1964. (S.C. Nash)

112. Sewage treatment works were once likely places to find narrow gauge railways; in south west London there were several in close proximity. The Wandle Valley Joint Sewerage Board had a works, now closed, at Merton, where 2ft 0in gauge Hudson-Hunslet 3097 (built originally in 1944 for the Ministry of Supply) is seen hauling a train of sewage sludge. When the railway system was superseded in 1963, this loco was acquired by the Brockham Museum, and subsequently became the inaugural (temporary) passenger loco at the Chalk Pits Museum. (C.G. Down)

113. In the Hogsmill valley, just south of Kingston-upon-Thames, no less than three sewage works, each with a separate 2ft 0in gauge railway, adjoined each other. At Surbiton works (the nearest to Berrylands main line station) can be seen Hibberd "Planet" diesel no. 2201 of 1939. This loco too was acquired for preservation when the railway system was closed. (C.G. Down)

115. Penfolds (Builders Merchants) Ltd extracted gravel from a pit at Eartham near Barnham. Amongst the small 2ft 0in gauge locomotive fleet was this rare type MD2 Orenstein & Koppel diesel (OK 7176). The perspective of this photograph makes it look doubtful if the locomotive could fit through the concrete tube "tunnel"! (C.G. Down)

←————

114. The City of Chichester Sewage Works was situated at Apuldram Lane south west of the city. Here another Hibberd loco operated, but of a rather different origin and design. Originally it had been built as a petrol loco by the Motor Rail & Tramcar Co for War Department Light Railway service. When World War I was over, a number of these machines were purchased by Hibberd (amongst others, including Motor Rail themselves) and at first resold with their petrol engines overhauled. By 1936, they were being sold with diesel engines (in this case by National Gas) and given "new" works numbers. Hibberd 1980 and much of the rest of the 2ft 0in gauge railway equipment became the first narrow gauge items at the Chalk Pits Museum. (C.G. Down)

116. The East Sussex Transport & Trading Co. extracted beach gravel until 1964 from Cuckmere Haven, between Newhaven and Eastbourne. A 2ft 0in gauge railway carried the gravel past the well known meanders of the Cuckmere to the main road at Exceat Bridge. Here an unidentified plate frame Motor Rail diesel of the 1930s poses, with a Southdown bus visible in the background. (G.E. Baddeley)

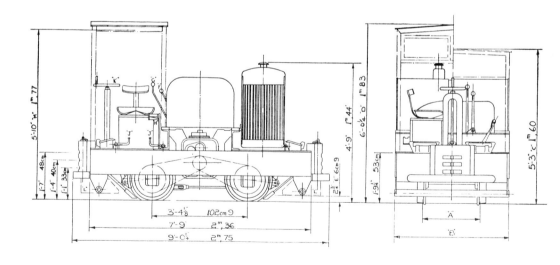

118. The main Hall & Co workshops were situated (and still are as part of the RMC group) at Washington, near Storrington in Sussex. Amongst the disused plant in 1962 was this class MM Orenstein & Koppel single cylinder petrol locomotive (OK 4588), another very rare machine. (C.G. Down)

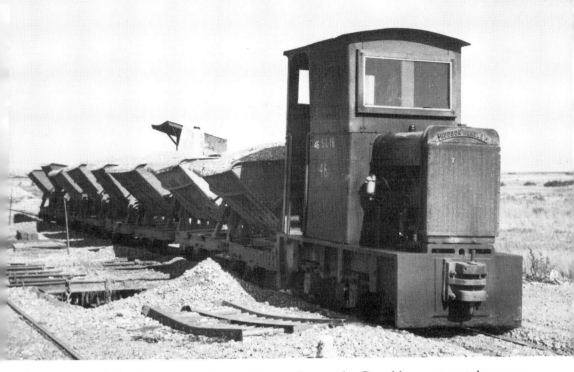

117. Just east of Eastbourne, another well known geographical feature, the Crumbles, provided the home for Hall & Co's gravel pits. Still in production today, the company formerly had a fleet of 2ft 0in gauge locomotives at the Crumbles; amongst them was no. 46/SL18, a standard Hudson-Hunslet diesel (HE 3587/48) fitted with a cab. (E.C. Griffith)

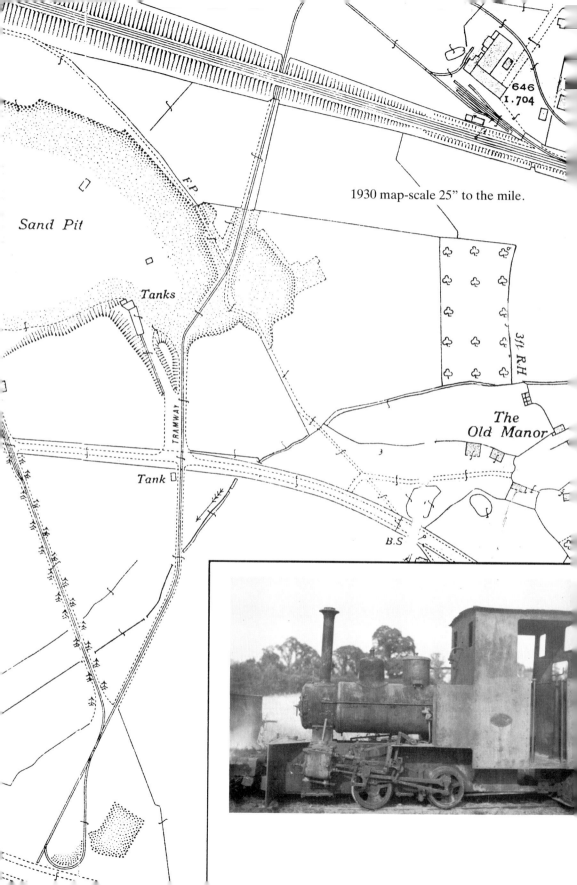

Sand Pit

Tanks

Tank

TRAMWAY

FP

1930 map-scale 25" to the mile.

3ft R.H

The
Old Manor

B.S

646
I.704

120. Pollock Brown & Co Ltd (a subsidiary of George Cohen) still operate a standard gauge line at Northam in Southampton. Until 1957, they had this Muir Hill locomotive (works no. L112), which is actually a standard Fordson tractor mounted on railway wheels! 21st October 1950. (J.H. Meredith)

←────────

119. The Buckland Sand & Silica Co near Reigate had, until 1952, a 2ft 0in gauge railway from BR worked private sidings, through the pits to the workshops alongside the A25 road. As well as six Motor Rail diesels, they possessed this tiny Hudswell Clarke class A 0–4–0 well tank (HC 1183/18) with cylinders only 5in x 8in. Originally supplied through Robert Hudson to Kidbrooke Aerodrome, it also worked on the construction of the Kingston by-pass before coming to Buckland. (D.H. Smith Collection)

Other Books from Middleton Press

BRANCH LINES

BRANCH LINES TO MIDHURST
Keith Smith & Vic Mitchell   *ISBN 0 906520 01 (*

Although the small town of Midhurst is only 50 miles from London, the three single railway lines that once served it
retained a rural character which is amply illustrated in this album. There is much evidence of the almost universal use
of steam locomotives together with diagrams and drawings of interest to modellers. Herein is ample material to
satisfy both the Southern Railway enthusiast and the lover of British Railway's steam branch lines.

BRANCH LINES TO HORSHAM
Vic Mitchell & Keith Smith   *ISBN 0 906520 02 9*

Although surrounded by electrified main lines the railways from Guildford and from Brighton to Horsham retained
their rural character which is fully portrayed in this album. Herein is ample material to satisfy both the Southern Railway enthusiast and the lover of British Railway's steam branch lines, whilst giving some insight into life in the locality
in bygone days.

BRANCH LINE TO SELSEY
Vic Mitchell & Keith Smith   *ISBN 0 906520 04 5*

For the local resident, this album shows in pictorial form the story of the local line whose coming brought about the
greatest period of development and prosperity the locality had ever known. For the railway lover, it illustrates a
quaint and unique tramway, portraying fully its charm and eccentric methods of operation. For the railway modeller,
every locomotive and type of coach is shown, together with track plans of each station.

BRANCH LINES TO EAST GRINSTEAD
Vic Mitchell & Keith Smith   *ISBN 0 906520 07 X*

The four branch lines, from each point of the compass, were typical rural railway byways, much loved by locals and
railway enthusiasts alike. They are comprehensively illustrated herein and their story is told in detailed captions,
together with 20 maps and a surprisingly humorous account of minor accidents.

BRANCH LINES TO ALTON (in preparation)
BRANCH LINE TO HAYLING (in preparation)

SOUTH COAST RAILWAY SERIES

BRIGHTON TO WORTHING
Vic Mitchell & Keith Smith   *ISBN 0 906520 03 7*

Much has been published on the London-Brighton part of the LBSCR. Herein the first section of the South Coast
line is examined in detail for the first time. The illustrations cover nearly 150 years and are of immense interest to
those interested in the development of the locality.

WORTHING TO CHICHESTER
Vic Mitchell & Keith Smith   *ISBN 0 906520 06 1*

One of the most significant chapters in local history is fully illustrated herein, with detailed maps of every inter-
mediate station. The wharves of Littlehampton and the day-trippers specials are just some of the subjects pictured
amongst the everyday railways scenes, past and present.

CHICHESTER TO PORTSMOUTH (in preparation)

OTHER SUSSEX BOOKS

MIDHURST TOWN – THEN AND NOW
Vic & Barbara Mitchell   *ISBN 0 906520 05 3*

The charming country town of Midhurst has been little affected by the passage of time, and this album fully portrays
its unique attraction with numerous illustrations from the past together with a few from the present for comparison.

GREEN ROOF OF SUSSEX
Charles Moore   *ISBN 0 906520 08 8*

A refreshing summer amble along the South Downs Way. You can sense the atmosphere – almost smell the wild
flowers and feel the birds swoop over your shoulder. A convenient way of walking 80 miles without leaving your
armchair.

OTHER RAILWAYS

WAR ON THE LINE
Bernard Darwin   *ISBN 0 906520 10 X*

The Southern Railway achieved remarkable transport feats after Dunkirk and suffered dreadfully in the Blitz, but its
greatest wartime undertaking was the movement of supplies for the Normandy landings. All this and more is
recounted in detail in this first reprint of the 1946 official story of the Southern in war-time.